A CIP catalogue record for this title is available from the British Library.

ISBN 9781399935517

Dedications

This book is dedicated to my daughters Cyla and Camryn. You are my everything and I will always be your biggest advocate. I want you to know just how special you are. I will forever be proud of you both.

For all girls out there, I want you to know that you are enough and whatever happens in life, be sure to spread a little kindness everywhere.

CeeCee loved school
and CeeCee always liked to be early...

She hated to be late for anything.

CeeCee was just like every other girl on the outside.

Only CeeCee didn't feel like it on the inside.

To everyone else CeeCee looked so happy and confident.

She loved

cheerleading,

gymnastics,

and dancing.

CeeCee was always on the go.

But CeeCee felt things that she didn't want anyone to know.

She often felt feelings of wetness down below.

CeeCee didn't tell a soul and the confident girl that everyone knew, just wasn't so.

The things that CeeCee felt, she would always hide, because she felt embarrassed and sad inside.

CeeCee felt all alone, the feelings she had just wouldn't go, in fact they just continued to grow.

She hated the way her clothes felt down below
and she was always worried in case everyone would see
if she had another wet show.

She would wiggle and jiggle but
the feeling still wouldn't go.

Some days she would cry,
and she didn't know why?

Other days,

she would **SHOUT** and **SCREAM!!!!**

...like she was stuck in a bad dream.

CeeCee didn't understand why...

Why was she different...

Why was this happening?

The wetness she felt was sometimes on her knickers.
But it was clear and smelt nothing like wee,
so what could it be?

It often made her
have a sore tummy.

Then one day, when CeeCee went to the loo, she saw spots of red on her knickers and tissue.

She didn't know what to do?

It looked like blood, but surely it couldn't be, so she rushed to tell her mummy and daddy.

CeeCee knew she had to
tell a grownup and
make them aware,
so together they
talked to help
her prepare.

CeeCee wasn't
different after all.

Her mum and dad told her that all girls get these feelings of wetness down below and so all girls should know that they must never feel alone.

Some girls do not notice it and some girls feel it a lot.

It will come and it will go,
but it eventually develops a pattern and a bit of a flow.

This thing that girls have, comes once a month.

It can stay for a day or as long as a week.

It can give some girls a tummy ache.

And makes some girls
want to sleep.

It can make some girls feel angry.

And makes some girls feel sad like they want to weep.

Some girls can have a little bit of redness called spotting and some girls can have a lot.

This is all completely normal.

CeeCee's mum and dad talked to her about hygiene and told her that you must always stay clean.

Girls can wear magic underwear or special pads in their knickers, that nobody else can see.

CeeCee felt better with all the new things she had learnt.

CeeCee's smile returned, and her confidence grew.

She was back to the old CeeCee that everyone knew.

These things that CeeCee has are called periods.

The redness in her knickers and on her tissue is blood.

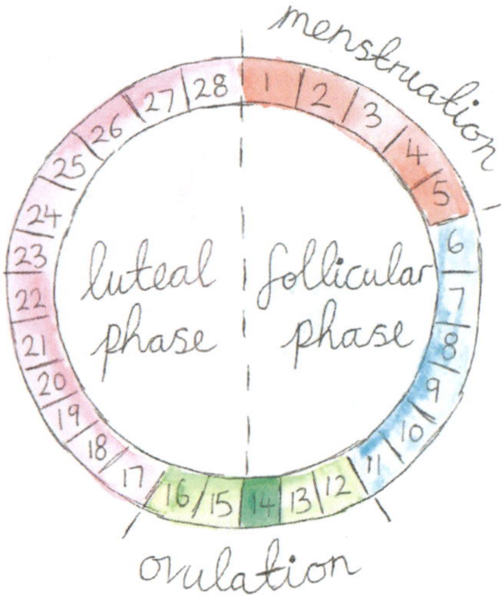

There is no need to be scared or embarrassed,
this is a normal part of every girl growing up.

Periods can start at any time, the average age is 9.
But some girls start earlier and some girls start later.

CeeCee started early,
but CeeCee always like to be early.
She hated to be late for anything.

Girls you must always remember
that you are never alone.
If you are worried about anything
then please speak to a grown up that you trust.

Period Tracker

	January	February	March	April	May	June	July	August	September	October	November	December
1												
2												
3												
4												
5												
6												
7												
8												
9												
10												
11												
12												
13												
14												
15												
16												
17												
18												
19												
20												
21												
22												
23												
24												
25												
26												
27												
28												
29												
30												
31												

Date	How am I feeling and where am I feeling it?

Chart Indicators

T	Tired
A	Angry
S	Sad
▲	Tummy Ache
✖	Headache
●	Acne
╱	Spotting
L	Light
H	Heavy

Get to know your body

Use this page to write down how you are feeling and where you are feeling it in your body.

Use the Period Tracker by inputting the chart indicators shown.

Use the colours, shapes, or letters to show the days you are feeling a certain way leading up to your period. Also note down how much bleeding you have using the indicators.

You will eventually begin to see a pattern from month to month.

Period Tracker

	January	February	March	April	May	June	July	August	September	October	November	December
1												
2												
3												
4												
5												
6												
7												
8												
9												
10												
11												
12												
13												
14												
15												
16												
17												
18												
19												
20												
21												
22												
23												
24												
25												
26												
27												
28												
29												
30												
31												

Date	How am I feeling and where am I feeling it?

Chart Indicators

T	Tired
A	Angry
S	Sad
▲	Tummy Ache
✖	Headache
●	Acne
╱	Spotting
L	Light
H	Heavy

Get to know your body

Use this page to write down how you are feeling and where you are feeling it in your body.

Use the Period Tracker by inputting the chart indicators shown.

Use the colours, shapes, or letters to show the days you are feeling a certain way leading up to your period. Also note down how much bleeding you have using the indicators.

You will eventually begin to see a pattern from month to month.

Printed in Great Britain
by Amazon

26534601R00018